My Pathway to Purpose

Dr. Barbara Butterfield-Jervis

MY PATHWAY TO PURPOSE

iUniverse books may be ordered through booksellers or by contacting:

iUniverse
1663 Liberty Drive
Bloomington, IN 47403
www.iuniverse.com
844-349-9409

ISBN: 978-1-6632-5806-9 (sc)
ISBN: 978-1-6632-6101-4 (hc)
ISBN: 978-1-6632-5807-6 (e)

Library of Congress Control Number: 2023921900

Print information available on the last page.

iUniverse rev. date: 03/04/2024

CONTENTS

I dedicate this book to my loving Heavenly Father,
Jesus Christ, for without Him I wouldn't be here today;

and to my wonderful daughter and only child,
Tarina, who is my inspiration—

I thank God that He chose to bring you into my life,
and I want you to be reminded always of how dear you are to me;

and in memory of my father, Lester Robert Butterfield,
who departed this life August 31, 2022, and who was involved
in most of my childhood journey and struggles.

FOREWORD

"Friendship is not about who you have known the longest. It's about who walked into your life and said, 'I'm here for you,' and proved it."

It has been a very insightful experience to know Dr. Barbara Jervis as a dear friend. I have known her for a very long time, but our friendship moved to another level when we attended a Woman, Thou Art Loosed conference, which was spiritually exhilarating.

I know Dr. Barbara as a prayer warrior, a God-fearing person, and a spiritually authentic person—someone who has a deep knowledge of God's Word and its application to daily living. She has committed her life entirely to God. Her youth work, the preaching of sermons, meditations, and previous writings have all been an inspiration to me.

As you read her thought-provoking life story and become aware of her struggles in life, particularly emotional and verbal abuse, may you be inspired and encouraged to embrace God's love and forgiveness. May you also know that through prayer, meditation, and the study of God's Word, you can indeed know His purpose for your life. As you grow in faith as she has done, may you too discover your pathway to purpose.

Congratulations to Dr. Barbara on another book, and lots of love.

The Reverend Dr. Julia E Williams

A MEMORIAL TRIBUTE TO MY FATHER

I made the following tribute to our Dada at his homegoing, September 2022. The written version is presented with minor changes for clarity.

I stand here today to celebrate the life of my dada, also known as Lester, Cash, and Tiger.

Life for us as children was not a perfect one. We had our share of rough times—one that today's world would call abusive. Instead our society would be a better place today.

My father was very protective of his three older girls. The way in which he expressed it seemed unfair to me—one to be feared, one that left me not wanting to associate myself with the opposite sex for fear of my dad.

Despite all of that, my dada loved his children. Fond memories for me as a child were the days of riding around in the big truck visiting his cousin Philistina Butterfield, driving along Front Street during the Christmas holidays to see the beautiful lights, and even hearing the knocks in the ceiling in every area of the house at night as he was killing mosquitoes. My Dada was a provider for his family. We cannot recall a day or night going without food. He was a provider for us even if it was from the "second shop"—our family's inside joke.

My dad loved to see us eating lots of food, and that trickled down to his grandkids. His famous words will remain with us until we leave this earth: "Eat while you got breath, cause isn't no eating after death." That started when he used to work at the naval base and took us there every Fourth of July for the American Independence celebration. Back then, as a child I used to go in the hot dog eating contest. "Eat while you got breath" is the only advice I'm sorry I obeyed, because I wouldn't have this size on me today if I hadn't!

Seeing my father, you would never imagine he was afraid of anything. I didn't until one rainy evening, when I walked out into the kitchen and there was Dada, this big, tall strapping man on top of the kitchen table, kneeling down with a broom in his hand, chasing away two small kittens who had found their way into the house. Up to this day, every time I think of that image it makes me laugh. He was afraid of cats!

As children we always knew when my dad was coming home. We'd hear him, his Spanish words, and we never knew if they were in order—phrases like "every dog in Georgia dead" and "broogadem bam." That was our dada.

Dada loved his country music so much so that the LPs and eight-track tapes in our home were overwhelming. I remember Temard and me playing his country tunes for him whilst he was ill, and the tears trickled down his cheeks as he listened and reminisced. "Play the songs," he'd say. That was our dada.

Dada's love was unconditional, especially for his grandchildren, and this is something I will cherish from his character and take with me forever. His kindness and generosity will be remembered by all who had the pleasure of knowing him. As I read the hundreds of condolence messages, he is referred to as a legend. He was a legend in his own right, and to us he is our only legend because there can only be one Dada.

Growing up, I could never imagine my life without my parents. There were times when I'd be somewhere sitting alone, and I'd sit and imagine it and cry. When he was a sailor, every time we went to church and they sang the hymn "Let the Lower Lights Be Burning," I would break down crying because he was away from us on the high seas sailing. On August 31, I lost my Dada at the age of eighty years. I'm fifty-seven, and it hurts really bad.

On September 9, eleven years ago, he and I had a heart-to-heart conversation about the way he treated me in my younger years, with tears streaming down his face whilst he was on his hospital bed as he looked at me in the presence of my mother and the late Villamay Daniel. I expressed to him how much I loved him and had forgiven him for those years. He looked at me and said, "Barbara, I want you to imagine yourself walking on a rocky road with a bucket of water on your head, and every time you bunk your toe, a little water will come out of the bucket. But when you reach home and you take the bucket off your head, you will still have water left there. So it was—that was the only way I could have expressed myself. Those hardships were because I wanted my children, especially my girls, to grow up being good girls. I wanted the best for you all." He cried some more, than he said to me, "Look at you today, look what type of life you have. I am proud of you, and that is all I wanted. Please forgive me."

Since that day, my dada and I had formed a bond, and when he got sick an even closer bond. During our quiet moments, we talked, and he confessed a lot of things to me and said that he was sorry and I must forgive him, which I assured him I did, years ago. If he didn't see me for a while, he would send a message to me via my daughter Tarina that he asked for me, and I would then find my way to Grand Turk to see him.

The lesson that I've learnt, and more so today, is that every circumstance I have faced and will face in my life is God's road map to get me to the purpose he has destined for me. He knew that one day He would need me to minister to my dad.

During the week leading up to his death, I was so happy that I had the chance of spending quality time with him, ministering to him one-on-one for several days, making sure he came back to God before leaving this earth. I say "come back," because my father was once a professing Christian, baptized in water, working fervently for the Lord in this same church, but he backslid. Throughout his illness, he was being ministered to, and he confessed that his heart had been right with God for the past year and a half. This is something that played heavily on my mind.

There was still one thing he needed to do to be sure he was ready to meet his Maker. I counselled him, and he said to me, "Barbara, I don't want to go to hell." I told him what he needed to do. On Sunday afternoon, August 28, 2022, he demonstrated his peace, and his soul became free. It was signed and sealed. After that, he said, "I am going," and when he was asked, "Where are you going?" he said, "To heaven." My eyes welled up with tears, and my heart was made glad because the mission was complete; he was ready to go.

As I left his bedside that afternoon to catch the flight back to Provo, I told him that I would be back and that I loved him. He replied, "I love you too." Those were the last four words I heard from my dada. If only I could hear your voice one more time!

To say I loved my dad would be an understatement, and to say I'm going to miss him would be an even greater understatement. But I am so incredibly grateful and happy that I can stand here today with the assurance that if I remain faithful to God, I will be reunited with him one day on that great getting-up morning.

I am grateful to God for my dad and my upbringing, because the life I had was only preparation for me to be able to be in the spiritual place in my life to minister to him during his last days on earth. You see, God's ways are not our ways, neither are His thoughts.

Not a day passes since you left us, Dada, that you don't cross my mind. Not all of you departed when you left this earth behind. In my heart there is a place that only you can hold, filled with loving memories more priceless than gold. I know you can still hear me in the spirit, Dada, so please know this is true, like I've told you whilst you were alive, over and over again: everything I am today is all because of God, Mama, and *you*.

I will always miss you, and you will always live on in my heart. Take your sweet rest.

INTRODUCTION

"For I know the plans I have for you," declares the Lord,
"plans to prosper you and not to harm you, plans
to give you hope and a future."
Jeremiah 29:11–12 NIV

There is a process you must go through before you come to realize what your purpose here actually is in the land of the living. It does not matter what your racial or social background may be; whether black, white, Caucasian, Hispanic, rich, or poor, we were all born with a purpose. Before we were created or conceived in our mother's womb, our Heavenly Father knew the plans He had for our lives.

What a difference it would make in the lives of the young men and women of today if they knew that they were created and born with a special purpose and that God has a specific and unique plan for their lives. I believe it would help them to endure the different situations they may face whilst on their path.

I know for myself that I almost destroyed my life, but because of the mercies of God I'm here because He kept me. I am here because He had ahold on my life and never let me go. From a troubled teenager, I have become a woman of purpose. During my earlier years I needed to know that there was more to life than just existing and that I had a purpose on this earth. If I'd had this knowledge then that I now possess, it would have literally set me free and given me hope for my life long before now. I hope someone reading this book will learn from my mistakes and my ignorance and as a result be encouraged and prepared to live a more accomplished and happy life.

Looking back, I see how God used my trying and challenging experiences as a teenager, along with my gifts and abilities, to give me a burden and a passion for youth. I always had a compassionate heart and an innate, burning desire to encourage them and give them hope and purpose through Jesus Christ—hope that I wish I'd had in my formative years and in recent times when I needed it most.

Many young people who made the decision to serve Christ are still serving the Lord years later. I can speak from my personal experience and declare that it took a lot of hard work and commitment. But it was well worth it.

As you live out your purpose, it is good to look at your history and background. Write down your past experiences, including the good and the bad, that have played a significant role in your life. God will use all of it to make you what He desires you to be. What is equally if not more important is that you *write down* the vision for your future. There is a saying that if you fail to plan, then you plan to fail. That is advice worth taking.

One of the first things we need to do is believe and know that God has a plan for our lives. As we read in Jeremiah 29:11 above, God already knows the plans He has for us. We just need to believe Him in unwavering faith and diligently seek Him in fervent prayer to find out what those divinely orchestrated plans are. Understand that God made you unique for a specific purpose, and there is no one on the planet who has the exact life experiences, gifts, talents, and abilities that you do. Just know that you were ordained by God for a unique purpose.

I truly believe that when we are faced with difficult and trying times, that is exactly when God is preparing us to be able to help someone else who may be going through what we went through or, as incredible as it may seem, are presently going through. His Word says that He will not put on us any more then we can bear but will give the strength to endure, and I know that's a fact. He prepares and strengthens us daily.

Today I can say that every road I trod was taking me to my purpose. There are times in our lives when we have our heart and mind set on a particular goal. We seek the Lord for His blessing and guidance; we ask Him to take control in leading us to that goal. Then He takes over and takes us to many pathways before we arrive. We sometimes wonder, "Why am I here at this point in my life when I'm supposed to be over there?" You see, I've learned that God's ways are not our ways, neither are His thoughts ours. You may be thinking you can go from point A then straight to B, but God sometimes takes us from A to G, Z, and Y before we arrive. Why? Because He has a purpose for every pathway He takes us on.

Even now in this present time, I am still faced with difficulties and trials that sometimes come upon me like a ton of bricks, but God helps me through them all. This life is not easy, especially not for those who are the called; you may be let down by people who are supposed to be looking out for you, and you are often used and abused. Life throws you a curve ball that you miss every time, but just as in baseball, you get to walk to first base, which begins your pathway. Then after the other batsman comes in and hits the ball far enough, which I will term your trials, you finally make it home, which I will call your purpose.

Before I begin detailing my pathway to purpose and sharing some of the things I've experienced, I wish to say that in no way do I mean any of these things to be degrading to anyone. I tell this story only for the purpose of helping others and to encourage others that God can give you beauty for any ashes that may be in your life. The trials you may face are only your pathway to purpose. This is my story.

CHAPTER 1

On a Thursday, March 11, 1965, I was born at home with a midwife of many years who had delivered hundreds of babies in just the way I was delivered. I was told that I was a very hairy baby, and there was something strange about my head; I was told that something grew on it after I was born. It looked as if I had another head that wanted to form, but with constant care and attention it went away after a couple of weeks.

I am the sixth of ten children, six boys and four girls. I am the second girl, and life for me was rough even before I came into the world. I believe that in every family there is one member whose life is the roughest. Growing up was rough for me. Throughout my childhood, I was content because I felt deep within that that was the way life was supposed to be for me. My parents starting going to church, and both of them professed Christianity. We had no choice but to be in church on Sunday morning and some evenings, Bible study on Tuesday and prayer meeting on Wednesday, and Sunday school. My life was a routine of school, house chores, house chores, house chores, and church.

When I think about the chores, my mind always goes back to washing dishes, washing clothes, ironing clothes, grocery shopping, and eventually cooking. Life seemed like it would be rough road, with me always being the one at fault whenever a rivalry or disagreement occurred. I would never be a favorite of anyone.

As a child I was very obedient, so obedient that one would have thought I was a robot, giving in to the wishes of everyone just to feel accepted. But that was only a tranquilizer for the moment when reality kicked in. Even as a child, it was always time for me to do the chores around the house, or clean up after my younger siblings and bathe them or change their diapers. Those were the days of scrubbing boards and coal irons. After washing so many loads of clothing and ironing uniforms for every one of us to wear to school for the entire week ahead, going to the store and shopping for groceries was a treat for me, although it sometimes included lifting heavy boxes or pushing a box cart, making several trips until all was carted home.

Evenings, especially on weekends, I would look forward to playing games such as hopscotch, marbles, jump rope, and rounders, which we know today as softball. It was customary then for a child not to be found in the road or at a neighbour's house when the sun set. I made the mistake one evening of coming home after the sun had gone down. I received such a lasting memory that I promised myself no matter where I might be or with whom, or whatever I was doing, I would never let the sun set on me again.

CHAPTER 2

At the tender age of four, I attended the government primary school named North School, now Ona Glinton Primary. Going to school had been a highlight of my earlier years amidst the pounding on our heads with a pencil and being called "dumb caps" by our kindergarten teacher. This took place every day. Eager to learn, I would always blank out her unkind remarks, which I know now would hinder a child from learning—being told by the teacher that upon our heads were "dumb caps."

After a few months went by, there came a change of that teacher for a teacher from the Volunteer Service Organization (VSO), who came to teach us from the United Kingdom. School was sheer joy under the tutelage of this lady.

At the end of the school term one year, during the Christmas break, we had our class party. Each of us was assigned an item to bring to the party. Because my mother was a baker, I was asked to bring a cake. My mother whipped up a yellow cake with raisins for me to take to the party. She was an excellent baker back then. On my way there, I was curious of how it tasted. Not being able to break a piece of it, I decided to pick the raisins that were visible and had a hearty taste before reaching to school with my donation.

Every weekend it was my duty to grease close to twenty bread tins as my mom got up during the early hours of the morning to loaf her bread to put in the oven for her numerous clients. It was how I am now able to make homemade bread.

Despite the unfair treatment I received at times, I personally had a close bond with my parents. I yearned for the love and attention that any child would want, but I was the least.

At church I was always attentive to the preaching of the Word of God. The crucifixion made me emotional whenever I saw a picture of Jesus being beaten or hanging from the cross. I would cry because I felt sorry for Him, but after learning why He died, that it was for me, I would cry because I could not imagine someone loving me so much as to even die for me. Although I knew all of that, I still did not have a relationship with God. I still was not saved.

In our home during those years, every morning my mom would gather all of us around her in the family room for morning devotions. It was there that I learned about the coming of the Lord. After hearing about it one morning, I went to school thinking about what our Bible study focused on that morning, and it never left me all day at school. I wasn't able to focus on my lessons. Instead, I cried and cried and cried for fear that when I arrived home my mom would be gone up in the Rapture. My teacher took me aside to try to calm me down. He questioned me about whether someone had done something to me or if I was feeling ill; I never gave him a response.

After school that day, my teacher accompanied me home and asked to speak to my mom. He told her how I cried at school all day and that he got no response from me. After he left our home, she asked me why I was crying. I told her how my mind was on what she said to us during the morning devotions about the coming of the Lord and that I knew I was not ready should the Lord have come that day, and I was afraid that when I arrived home she would be gone. I told her I wanted to be saved, but she did not lead me to the Lord at that moment. It was not until I went to church on Sunday, after the Word was preached, that I walked the aisle of the Bible Baptist Church and gave my heart to the Lord at the tender age of nine. I was led to the Lord by the pastor's wife. It was the month of October, and on my birthday the following year, on March 11, 1975, I was baptized after church on Resurrection Sunday.

Going to church was a delight for me after accepting the Lord. I enjoyed memorizing the scriptures for Bible study, then standing up in front of the congregation reciting what I learned and giving my group lots of points. As a young Christian, I thoroughly enjoyed reading the Word and praying on a daily basis. I wanted to know all I could about the Lord.

During those times, I started having dreams and would hear a voice talking in my head about what would happen, and if I'd dreamed it, I would see it come true. I would tell my siblings about what I was seeing in my dreams, and when these things would come true they all would call me a witch. Now I know that it was the Holy Spirit speaking to me.

CHAPTER 3

I was very young when I entered the government school system. At the age of ten, entering grade five, I ended up in a class of children that was three or four years older. I felt like a rose among thorns because they were more experienced and would have me as the baby of the group.

It was that year when my class had to prepare for the Common Entrance Test to enter high school. I was very intelligent and never came below second in my class when there was an exam. When the time came and we sat the exam, I was the only one in my class who had passed for high school that year. My teacher felt very bad but said I was the only one she had confidence in when we sat the exam.

The year I entered high school, I was so slender that my uniforms would not fit me properly. I wasted a lot of my high school years, and I think it came from the mere fact that I had a problem understanding the teachers who were appointed to teach. Ninety percent of them originated from India.

Those were the days when we would go home for lunch and you had to get back before the bell rang. I remember vividly eating bread and sugar and water. The water was sweetened with sugar, and, oh, that was so refreshing, especially on a hot sunny day.

Among the group of students I was placed with, I became fond of a few and would look to them for acceptance—acceptance that one day caused my entire life to change emotionally.

One day after school was dismissed, as three of my friends and I were walking home from school, it began to rain. The father of one of my friends sometimes picked her up after school to take her home. Seeing us all walking in the rain, he stopped and picked us up as well. That ride changed my life emotionally.

I lived in the area called West Road, and all the others lived in the area called Over Back. My friend's father, who is now deceased, dropped all of them home first. I was the last one to be dropped home. Whilst driving me home, he placed his hand under my blue uniform skirt, into my underwear, and molested me.

That was a moment I shall never forget. I thought my life would end that very moment. I felt so afraid and devastated; I sat there and cried and wanted to die. It was in an era when you were told that after you begin menstruating, or as some would say "begin seeing your period," if a boy even touched you in that area with his hand, you would get pregnant.

At the end of the ride and one of the worst moments in my young life, I pulled myself together and went into the house. I was afraid to tell my mom what had just happened to me because I knew I would have been blamed for it happening to me and would have been beaten.

I hardly ate my food that evening. I went to bed very early and just cried all night, holding my stomach for fear that I was pregnant, because of what I had been told. This crying continued for many months until I realized that my monthly flow was still coming. I knew it was a sign that I was not having a child for this horrible man who had destroyed me emotionally.

When I would see him almost every day and he would stop to offer me a ride home from school, I would not even look at him. I was afraid of him, hated him, and felt like killing him for what he did to me. This was a secret I lived with for many, many years. The only person who knew—because He is all-knowing—was my only true friend and confidant, Jesus, to whom I prayed every day and almost all day about it.

This experience made me feel like I was dirty, and when I was being abused physically by my dad, I used to think about it and felt like I deserved being beaten. From the tender age of eleven years, I started developing low self-esteem. During the night I had many nightmares and often felt like I was losing my mind, along with other difficult experiences I got daily. Being treated like I was not important was taking a mental toll on me.

This experience made it very difficult for me to concentrate on my school work. I had a hard time comprehending what was taught, and I went through high school just going through the motions.

I can testify that sexual molestation is a traumatic experience that can have long-lasting effects on a person's mental health and well-being. If you have experienced sexual molestation as a child and have not told anyone, it can be a heavy burden to carry.

If you have been sexually molested as a child and not told anyone, it is important to acknowledge your feelings. It is common to feel a wide range of emotions when you've been sexually molested, such as shame, guilt, fear, anger, and sadness. If I had known it then, I would not have let it cause me to fall into a state of low self-esteem. I would have accepted these emotions, knowing that they are a normal reaction to an abnormal situation.

I was young, and therefore I did not know to seek professional help, which is important to seek if you've been sexually molested. Finding someone to help me process my emotions, work through trauma, and develop coping strategies could have made this path a little easier. It would have helped me to address the mental health issues that arose as a result of the abuse.

Today, I would advise anyone who was molested to consider reporting the abuse. Reporting sexual abuse can be a difficult decision, but it can also be empowering. Reporting the abuse can help protect others from the perpetrator and can provide a sense of justice. If you decide to report the abuse, it's important to have a support system in place and to seek legal advice.

Dealing with sexual molestation as a child and not telling anyone can be a difficult and lonely experience. It's important to acknowledge your feelings, seek professional help, join a support group, practice self-care, find a safe outlet, and consider reporting the abuse. Remember that healing takes time, but with the right support it is possible to recover and live a fulfilling life.

CHAPTER 4

After my five years in high school, it was time for graduation. Besides my personal problems, the class was faced with all kinds of problems leading up to graduation. These ranged from the shortage of teachers, to demonstrations staged by parents and students, to a change of the education administration. The GPA for graduation was set higher as a payback, leaving 90 percent of the class graduating with only a school leaving certificate.

Right after I sat my exams, I sought employment to teach at a private school on the island. This school was affiliated with the church I was attending at the time. I was taken on staff to teach and was paid as a missionary in the amount of $130 per month.

About three weeks before my graduation, my mom fell ill, which was devastating for me as I had been looking forward to graduation. She was hospitalized for her illness and was bedridden for a while. What a blow for us, looking forward to graduation, and here we were with no money to get our dresses and shoes for this important time in our lives.

Being the kind, compassionate person I was, I took all my little savings from my teaching job, bought material, and got one of the best seamstresses to sew our dresses for the valedictory service. We were able to buy shoes, pantyhose, and everything for the service.

A very dear friend of mine told me that she would help me dress for the service, and if I may say, she transformed this then-slender young lady. I looked beautiful on that day, and it was my first time wearing makeup.

Before going to the service, they took me to the hospital for my mom to see me. I must say, seeing her lying there in the bed and not being able to attend our service made me cry. We attended the service, the graduation ceremony, and all the other activities that were held for our graduation whilst my mom was still hospitalized.

I continued teaching at the school and thoroughly enjoyed it. I looked forward to interacting with the children who were in my class. I was complimented by parents for the vast improvement they saw in their children's work. Teaching was my passion. I wanted it to be my ambition when I left school, but because of the way our education system was structured, I was placed in a group during my fourth year that they thought would be good clerical officers and secretaries. This broke my heart, and I felt like I could not pursue my teaching anymore.

But despite that, I have never regretted teaching for that early period in my life, when I was fifteen years old. It was how I hid from the pain I was in.

CHAPTER 5

My work life started very young. I left teaching at the school after securing a job in the government service. I spent most of my time attending church. I would eagerly await the bus that picked us up for service. As difficulties prevailed at home, I was challenged for going to church. After the church I was attending split up, 90 percent of the people left, including my mom. As a child I did the same and starting attending another church.

I had a love for singing in my younger years, and I was honored to join a gospel singing group called the Mighty Stars of Harmony. I really enjoyed being a part of that group. My first solo was "If I had it to do all over again, I'll serve Jesus every day of my life." That song meant a lot to me then, and it still does now.

We travelled the Turks and Caicos Islands, holding concerts. In 1984 we travelled to Miami Beach, Florida, and recorded an album, which was an accomplishment for me. This was my first trip to the United States, and I must say it was an experience out of this world.

Although this ministry was joy for me, at home it was a problem. It is so sad to see how something good counted as bad in a child's life. It was felt that I had other "motives" whenever I would leave the house to go to our practice sessions.

I remember one weekend we went to Providenciales to hold concerts during the weekend. Our way of transportation there was the police boat. After hours on the boat, we arrived safely that Saturday. We left there on the Monday, which was a public holiday. The trip back home turned into a frightening experience when we got lost at sea, in the middle of the ocean at night. Not knowing where we were, we toiled most of the night.

I found myself thinking, "Hey, if this boat goes under, I have no reason to live." I had made up my mind to die; I was living only to get abused physically and verbally, and it was taking a toll on me mentally. If I died that night, I would be going home to heaven.

And so it was that when we got help and were able to come ashore safely, I felt somehow disappointed. A lot of people from the community were at the waterfront to greet us. They were happy, but I was sad.

My life changed during those three years. One might think that, at the age of seventeen, I would be thinking about getting a boyfriend, but that was not me. If any guy approached me, I would literally run away from him, although there was a part of me that wanted to be loved and accepted.

This went on for a while, until one day a guy set a trap in order to talk to me, and I gave in to him. We talked for a few days, then I decided to give the relationship a try. At this stage in my life, the physical challenges were growing worse. If I was seen talking to my boyfriend, that meant consequences when I got home. I can remember running and ducking so that I wouldn't be seen in public because of what I would receive.

I attended prayer meetings and revival services on a regular basis just to get away, most of the time, and to see my boyfriend. Unfortunately, fornication became a part of that relationship, and I ended up in a backslidden condition. I knew that I truly was born again because at times when I was engaging in fornication, I would hear a voice speaking loudly in my mind, saying, "This is not what I want for you. You are mine; you need to get out of this relationship." I was so nervous and afraid when this happened. Afterward I would cry and pray asking forgiveness, but I continued with it because I thought that I was loved. This was someone who cared for me, or so I thought.

CHAPTER 6

Although I was in this relationship, the pressures of life were still pressing down on me mentally. At home I would spend most of my time in my bedroom.

There was a sister in the church with whom I became very close, and at times I told her what I was going through. When I was in my room, crying and asking God questions, she would call me and minister to me over the phone.

I developed such low self-esteem that I thought no good would ever come to me. This went on for several months. I wanted so much to go home to God. I asked for forgiveness of my sins each night before I went to sleep. I knew I was not living a holy life while committing fornication.

One Friday night when I had gone to bed early, I remember clearly that after I went off to sleep, I found myself in this beautiful place. There was a meadow, and the grass was so green. Across the meadow I saw a large tree. The breeze that blew from under that tree felt so good, and I decided I would go under that tree to sit down.

As I began to walk across the meadow, I realized there was a river flowing along it, and in order for me to get to the tree, I had to step into the river to cross over. I didn't hesitate, but just as I put one foot in the river to cross, my father began banging on the kitchen door, and I came back.

I felt so angry because as I thought about it, I knew I had been dying. That place felt so serene, with no cares of this world at all. When I shared this dream with persons from the church, they told me that I probably was dying. I knew that and was disappointed I hadn't. Later on, I read a passage in the book of Revelation where a tree and a river confirmed to me that I had been going home to Jesus.

There was no end to my problems, and I just wanted to leave this earth. One Saturday I went in the room I used to occupy with a rope and decided that this was the night. I would choke myself to death in the room.

But God had ordained it that one of my older brothers, who did not live with us, had come to visit as he did every weekend. Instead of stopping in the kitchen to talk with my mom, he came straight into the room where I was. I had already started trying to kill myself. He took the rope from around my neck and saved me from dying.

He immediately called my mom and told her what I was doing. She scolded me and told me she was calling the police on me for trying to kill myself. That was when I learned that I would have gone to hell for committing suicide.

CHAPTER 7

This was a turning point in my life. I realized that although I had a relationship with a guy, I still was not happy. There was emptiness, a void that needed to be filled.

After a while, he was no longer faithful to me and fell in love with one of my friends. His attitude toward me changed a lot, and he had started treating me very differently. This hurt me a lot.

That year, the Turks and Caicos business college opened. I attended to pursue a secretarial course. I had an urge to learn more of what I was doing on my job.

At school one day, I heard a lot of people talking about a revival that was being held at a church. Everyone was talking about the young preacher who was calling people up and telling them things that were happening in their lives. I decided I would go there out of curiosity on one of the nights.

That very same week, one day I found I could hardly walk because of pain in my right knee. I did not know why it was hurting me. I limped around most of the day, and after class that evening I decided I would go to the service. I got there early and slipped into a seat in the back. As the service went on, I just watched because I was not used to the clapping and shouting and noise. I came from a church that was very solemn.

The time for preaching came. When I saw the preacher, he looked as young as I was, and when he introduced himself I found that we were in fact of the same age. He preached and preached. As he was preaching, I hung my head, weeping and praying, asking God to forgive me of my sins and take me back to my first love. These were the exact words I prayed: "Lord, please take me back to my first love where I belong. Take me back, Lord."

At the end of his preaching, the young man gave an altar call. He began to call people up to the altar and started telling them things, and the people were crying. I began to get scared. Then he said, "There is someone in here whose right knee was hurting them all day. I want them to come up to the altar now."

My heart started beating so fast that I was hearing it in my head. I was praying someone else would move, but no one did. I said in my mind, *I am not going up there.*

Then he repeated the same thing and added, "This person is saying they aren't coming. I am going to count from ten to zero."

I was so terrified. He began to count, and when he got to two, I still sat there. Then he began dividing the one into fractions before going to zero. Before he reached zero, he said, "Your entire life depends on this."

Just before he could say zero, I jumped up and went to the altar. When I got there, he talked to me about my knee. Then he began to pray for my complaint. As he was praying, he began to speak in an unknown language which I know now was in tongues. Then suddenly he stopped. He said to me, "The Lord said I am to sing this song to you." And he began to sing, "Take me back, take me back dear Lord, to the place where I first received you." Boy, didn't I cry! This was exactly what I had been praying, and now there's this preacher telling me the exact same thing.

I repented and went back to God that night. That was my first encounter with the Holy Ghost. My life was never the same from that night. I became actively involved in the church in the youth department and as a member of their choir and a Sunday school teacher.

CHAPTER 8

Life in Christ went well for me for a couple of months with no fornication—my former boyfriend had gotten so serious with my friend that she got pregnant for him and he was paying attention just to her.

I did not go after him, as was custom in those days when a boy left a girl. But later on, when her family found out she was pregnant, they sent her to family abroad. After that was done, he came back after me. I played around for a while but still ended up getting involved with him again.

About a year later, he decided he was going off to school, so I did the same. It was my heart's desire to further my education. He went to Jamaica, and I went to Barbados. Going off to school was also an avenue for getting away from my problems at home and the hard housework I used to do.

Financially, my mom wasn't able to help me to go off to school, with so many children to take care of. But God always places persons in your life for times and seasons. With the help of a colleague, I was able to get a student loan from the development board, now named Turks and Caicos Islands Investment Agency. I saw God work for me in providing and opening doors, and I thank God for my colleague, who packed a bag of toiletries and other necessities for me to take to Barbados.

The trip to Miami was horrifying for me because I knew I would have to be away from home on my own for the entire two years. I wouldn't even talk about the flight to Barbados. There were other girls from home who went to the same college as I, and we contacted each other and arranged to travel on the same flight. I cried the whole trip.

The first weeks in Barbados were very hard for me. As much as I wanted to leave home so badly, I missed being home. I would cry like a baby to go back home. When I called home to talk to my mom, I would be crying uncontrollably because I missed her. I tried to settle in somehow because I knew I had gone to Barbados to further my education.

That first year with the girls was not nice for me at all. I was not treated well. The first week I was lied on and treated like a stranger. There I was in a strange land, having to face another chapter of bad treatment in my life. I ended up getting an apartment by myself, in St. Michael across from the Governor General's residence, and that was scary also.

Despite all that I went through, God was still with me. I knew what I had to do, so that is what I did. My first step was to find a place of worship. After shopping around, I found the right one just a twenty-minute walk from where I lived.

Walking to church one day, I met up with two young ladies. We became very friendly later on and have remained friends to the present. I got actively involved in that church, becoming a part of their sixty-member youth choir.

My first year at St. Caroline's Business College, I pursued the general secretary course. I enjoyed my classes and assignments, but I often met with some difficulty in shorthand. Along with shorthand, I was also faced with not having enough finances to maintain myself. The amount of money sent to me was a mere $500 every three months. My rent was $200 per month, which did include utilities. Food was a challenge for me to find, and I had many nights of going to bed with only water in my stomach.

Calling home for money would not do because they had none to send me, and my mom would get distraught when she asked if I had something to eat and I would answer no.

It was several weeks in Barbados before I touched base with my boyfriend. I cried then too because I still wanted to go home. I tried to bury myself in my school work and in going to church. I decided that no matter what I would place God and church first. A friend I made at St. Caroline's used to invite me over to spend weekends, and she would never let me leave unless she gave me a bag of groceries to last for at least a week.

The first holiday was approaching, Christmas. All the students from home were calling their parents to send them their tickets to be with them for this wonderful time of the year. When I called home, I was told I would have to spend Christmas in Barbados because there was no money to send me to come home. I was devastated and wept like a baby.

I felt horribly alone in a place where I had made few friends. On Christmas Eve I sat in the back of their vehicle and went to town with them. I watched people moving here and there shopping. I had no money, so shopping was not an option for me. I cried that evening uncontrollably as I was imagining how it was at home.

In my community, people usually went to church on Christmas morning, and so did I. Later that day, I was invited to the residence of a family who originated from Turks and Caicos but had lived in Barbados all their lives. The gathering was good, with lots of other people who were total strangers to me. At least I had a good Christmas meal that day.

As January rolled by, I waited patiently for the others to come back from home, just to hear something about what was happening at home. I had hoped to get something from my family, but nothing came. I knew I needed to get used to that.

As we entered the spring semester, work became a lot more difficult, but I loved the subjects, especially office administration. I looked forward to weekends when we were given assignments. I mastered typewriting and the shorthand practical. Shorthand theory was more difficult at this new level, but I knew I had to try hard.

I had to pass shorthand in order to qualify as a general secretary and then move on to my second year for the advanced course.

Times got even harder for me financially, many nights and days without food. I survived on flour and water, fried without vegetable oil. I did not want to depend too much on my friend, but sometimes I had no other choice.

At the end of the first year came time for exams. I studied all I could while concentrating on my shorthand theory. I got so nervous that I could hardly concentrate, but I tried my best.

The day came when I had to go to the office to collect my results. With sweating palms, I opened my slip, and my heart broke when I saw I had failed my shorthand theory by three points. I was told that in a week's time I could resit the subject. I studied and practiced so hard for the entire week. I needed to pass. I kept saying to myself that I had gone through too much not to pass my first year.

On Tuesday the following week I went to resit the exam along with a few others who also had to resit it. I made sure to pray before I started. When I was handed the exam, as calmly as I could I did every section, making sure I gained enough marks. I was told I could come the next day for the results.

I had prayed and asked God to help me pass, and I was totally depending on Him to see me through. I waited eagerly for the clerk to hand me my slip. When I opened it, I rejoiced to see my results. I had passed!

Attending the graduation was optional. Owing to my lack of finances, I decided not to attend. I had already asked my mom to try to send me a ticket to come home for the summer. I thought I would die if I didn't go home for such a long time.

I received my certificate in general secretarial studies, which was a great accomplishment for me. I called home that day to enquire if I would be getting the money to buy a ticket, and when I was told yes, I was so happy that I walked straight to Bridgetown that very day to make the reservations. The next day my money came, and I purchased my ticket.

The day I arrived home, I surprised my mother by going to her workplace. They announced that someone was there to see her. When she came out and saw me, she was so surprised. I felt so proud to hand her my diploma, which she carried around to show everyone on her job what I had accomplished.

CHAPTER 9

Summer at home was very much enjoyable time. I had managed to get a job while home, which allowed me to save a few dollars to take back with me.

During the break I was very active in our youth fellowship and other church activities. My fellowship with God was good because I was free of my boyfriend, who did not come home for summer. I was convinced that he had another girlfriend there in Jamaica, which would not have surprised me because he had done it to me before.

The day came when I had to leave for my second year. I had pursued finances for my second year to do the advanced secretarial course. One might think that after such a hard year financially I would have settled for just the first-year diploma, as many others did. But I had a determination to finish what I had started, and succeeded in securing the student loan after being successful the first year.

The experience of leaving home again was not as dramatic as the first time. Another girl was leaving for Barbados to go the same school, and we had decided to live together. I'd now have a roommate, so it should not have been as bad for me financially. But as it turned out, my second year was worse than the first. Thank God I had a friend to depend on at times for food.

I use to get a lot of phone calls from home those days. One evening, quite late at night, I was told I had a call, and when I went to the phone, it was my mom on the other end, telling me my grand-aunt had died. I felt so bad because I had not seen her before I left home. It almost felt like she was hiding from me, and since the time was against me, I had to leave for the airport without seeing her.

The day they buried her, I stayed in bed and wept the whole day. I felt so sad because I was not at home to see her remains being buried.

I enjoyed my school days, having other subjects including accounts, which I mastered. My church life became more active as I grew closer with the two girls attending the same church. There were days I would go and have dinner with them, which I really enjoyed. Their mom and dad treated me like I was their own child. But there came a time when I didn't want to be totally dependent on them.

My roommate was not a professing Christian, and she attended service with me only now and then. I would never put anything before my going to service. My relationship with God was growing in leaps and bounds. I was promoted to the big choir to take part in a presentation held at that church every Christmas. There were nights of practice sessions that went on for weeks.

When there was an exam I had to prepare for, I did not stay home, but when I went to bed at night, in my dreams I would see and hear my teachers lecturing me and explaining my work. For one exam in particular, I remember my roommate staying up all night studying, but when I came home from church, I went to bed. The next day we sat the exam, and when the results came out, she got 60 percent and I got 95. She was so upset! "I really don't understand this," she said to me. "You are always going to church and don't study, and I am up studying all night. Then when it's exam time, you always get better marks than me."

The key to my success was the scripture that says, "Seek ye first the kingdom of God and all His righteousness and all other things shall be added unto you." She'd never understand that because she was not saved.

My financial situation was horrible, and there came a time when I fell sick and did not have a penny to see a doctor. Thanks to a friend who loaned me some money to go to the clinic, the doctors told me I needed surgery because they saw a cyst on my ovary. It was very painful for me.

The church I was attending used to hold what they called a miracle service every Thursday morning. I looked forward to attending these services because I was free from classes on that day and I loved going to church. During one particular service, I was trusting God for finances, and a doctor came from one end of the building to the other where I sat. He said that God told him to give me something, and then he handed me fifty dollars. This truly was a miracle for me because I had just placed my last two dollars in the offering plate.

God proved himself to me that day. I knew that man could not have heard my prayer, as the building was so huge—it housed about three hundred people, and so many people attended that they used to have two services in the morning and two in the evening to accommodate everyone.

I still had no money for the surgery, so the only thing I could do then was trust God to heal me. At the service I placed my request before the Lord. When I went to the clinic the next week before they scheduled the surgery, they decided to do another test and found out that the cyst had disappeared. I was so excited I testified to my miracle at the next Sunday service. Praise the Lord! God came through for me, again.

Another time was when my roommate and I had nothing to eat, but there was a banana tree in our backyard. We ate bananas just off the tree, we mixed banana with flour and fried it or baked it.

One Sunday when I was in church I felt so hungry and kept praying for God to provide something for us to eat that day. Before I left home, the only thing we had was rice. I told my roommate to cook the rice for when I got back. She asked, "What are we going to eat with it?" I told her God would provide.

After the service I was so hungry that I breathed in the aroma of the neighbourhood food cooking. I prayed and trusted God. When I arrived home, the only thing there was the rice. I was home for about fifteen minutes when our doorbell rang. I ran to it because I knew that was the answer to my prayer.

Our landlord used to come by and ask me to type for him. There he was at the door with something he wanted typed. Before, he had never brought his own paper—I had always used mine. But that day, he brought me half of a pack of paper. God knew I had none for school the next day. After the landlord had handed me the paper and left, I saw that there was an envelope. I opened it and found eighty dollars.

I hurried upstairs and danced before the Lord. My roommate wanted to know what had happened. I told her that after I typed the letters for our landlord, we would be going to a store to buy food. She was shocked and laughed. That day she and I had white rice, corn, and steak for dinner. We also bought something to drink and for dessert.

My relationship with God was close. I would dream of things, and they would come true. In one vision I had one night, I saw my mom sitting in a chair with her head held back, and someone behind her, washing her hair. I called home the next day and was told she had been feeling sick and had to be airlifted to Nassau. She had used some hair dye that did not agree with her scalp, and she was in critical condition. I was devastated and cried. I was so happy when I heard she was all right.

In February of that year, my mom phoned to tell me that my grandmother, whom I had never had the chance to see in all my life, was sick with cancer and dying. I told her I was expecting a cheque from my scholarship loan and would go to Freeport during the Easter break to see her before she died. Unfortunately, she died before the time came for me to leave. When Easter break came, I travelled for her burial. I was sad because I had really wanted to see her alive. Instead my first time seeing her was in the funeral home, laid out on a table, naked, and waiting to be dressed for her burial.

After the Easter break, the end of the school year was nearing, and exams were upon us. I continued going to church because I would soon be leaving Barbados and did not know when I would be able to visit again.

At the end of my last year, I graduated with a distinction diploma in secretarial studies. I was able to attend the graduation and was so excited to be going home, although it was bittersweet after bonding with my friends' family.

The Sunday before I left, I was selected to do a lead part in the choir. The night before I left Barbados, they surprised me with a bon voyage party. There was lots of food and drink, and I received a lot of gifts.

The parting with that family was sad. They came to see me leave, and I will never forget the look on their faces as I went to board the flight back home.

CHAPTER 10

I was excited getting off the flight that Friday. This time, my mom knew when I would be arriving, and I was met at the airport.

Here I was, back to the nest I had escaped from for two long, hard, yet fruitful years. I wondered, seeing that I had lived away for two years, how things must have changed. I would be happy now; at least that was what I thought. But rivalry among siblings prevailed, and I was always the one who was accused of starting it. Through life, I came to realize that jealousy is a tool that can kill you.

I was excited, though, because here I was, a qualified secretary who wanted a good job to support myself. I was able to secure a job back in government in the Social Welfare Department, which I really enjoyed. My tenure there afforded me the opportunity to become involved actively in the planning of National Youth Day, and I continued to fight for the youth of the Turks and Caicos Islands. I was one of those persons who secured the public holiday named National Youth Day!

The civil service was looking to fill the post of personal secretary to the Governor while his secretary was off for several months tending to her sick and ailing husband. After a thorough search was made, I was selected for the temporary position. One of the qualifications for this appointment was shorthand. I was qualified because in my second year I had done very well, and the only thing I had to do was dictation, which I enjoyed.

Several weeks after I came back home, my boyfriend returned. We had been estranged for a long time. I really did not bother me that we had lost track of each other. I was into the church and had already taken up the position of president of the youth fellowship.

After a while, we decided to rekindle the relationship. This road I began to walk was no different from before. But one day as I was walking to work, I distinctly heard a loud, loud voice speaking to me from the sky, saying, "He is not for you. This is not what I want for your life." I became so afraid; I looked around to see if someone was trying to scare me, but no one was in sight.

I began running, and when I got to work, I shared what happened with my co-worker, with whom I had become very close. She told me it was God speaking to me about my relationship and that I had better be obedient.

CHAPTER 11

Obedience was not the road I took. I continued on as the president of the youth department and also formed a youth choir in the church. My ministry was blooming. A lot of young people joined the youth fellowship and the choir. We purchased robes and held a lot of concerts and sang during the services. I took the choir on a trip to sing at the youth conference one year, and it was an awesome experience for us.

For Youth Sunday, I was asked to lead the service from time to time, and in doing so I knew my life had become one of fornication. I had been home a year now, and from the day when I was disobedient to the call of God on my life, I had been engaged constantly in fornication. I thank God He didn't take me out during that period in my life.

I remember vividly going to the doctor after missing my monthly and feeling sick, especially in the morning. I was told to take a test, and after returning the following day learned I was pregnant. My whole life changed instantly.

Every lunch break my boyfriend and I would meet and buy lunch. After going to the doctor that day, I told him I was pregnant. He was not enthusiastic at all, but eventually he came around and accepted it.

Afraid of what would happen to me at home, and ashamed because I was in charge of the young people, I kept saying to myself, "What am I going to say to these young people and my pastor?"

I mustered up the courage one day to meet with him and inform him what had happened to me. I was removed from my positions and put out of the church. I felt so embarrassed. I said to myself that I would never tell them at home, but eventually they all noticed. I went through hell then for it. Every morning I would get so sick and vomit up everything I ate. It was horrible the first two months.

My boyfriend started coming around our gate to see me but was not allowed to enter because of the strictness of my parents. I had stopped going to church because of shame and embarrassment of being put out and that I was pregnant out of wedlock, which was against my religion. Every Sunday I would find myself at the beach with him and then right back home.

When I was going into my third month, he came by one night and announced that he was moving out of his mom's house and going to live in an apartment. I got excited then because I thought he was getting ready to marry me. I never asked the question though. Then he blurted out that he was going to be sharing it with a lady! I was shocked and asked him who she was. Then I asked him how many bedrooms the place had, and he told me one.

I got angry instantly and asked where he would be sleeping. He said the sofa. I knew better, but he thought I believed him because he knew I loved him and had no choice other than to take what he was saying or leave it. We argued about this situation for a while, and soon he stopped coming by to see how I was doing.

I managed to tell a friend of his that I wanted to see him, and that evening he came by. We talked, and I asked him why I did not see him anymore. He said he was too busy. In other words, he told me nothing. I was puzzled. From that day, the only time I saw him was in passing on the road.

I was devastated. Here I was with this man's child in me, and he did not want anything to do with me. I grew so desperate one night that I went to his apartment, and his friend chased me from the door. He was right in the apartment and never came out to my defence.

From that day, I never went after him again. My pregnancy was a lonely one. Despite it, I still hungered after God and became attached to an older lady from my church. I started attending her prayer meetings that she held at home. Her home became my hiding place until one day her adopted daughter told me that her mother had told her not to be with me because I was pregnant and was a bad example for her. I didn't blame the lady though—I knew I had let the young people down as their youth leader.

I felt very bad because I was rejected by my family, my boyfriend, and now the lady to whom I had attached myself. My only haven was home, work, and a friend from my childhood days.

One day at the clinic, I was told I had developed high blood pressure. The doctor asked me if I was worrying or going through problems. I told her yes, and she advised me that I was putting my life and that of the baby in danger. But it was hard not to worry. I was so alone. I stood at our gate each night, hoping my boyfriend would change his mind and come back to me, but he never did. My blood pressure was out of control, and I was hospitalized for a week before I could be discharged.

One Sunday evening I decided to go to church. Although I was in that state, I still had a desire to live for God. At the end of the service when the altar call was made, I walked the aisle with my stomach as big as ever and went back to the Lord.

After a while I started going back to the home of the lady from my church home for prayer. One evening when we were having prayer, I felt my underwear wet. I went home and told my mom, and she told me my water probably had broken and I had to wait on the pains.

For several days, no pains came, and I was not taken to the hospital. Upon visiting clinic one day, I was sent straight to the hospital. It was the first week in April. I thought that if my child's father found out that I was hospitalized, he would come to look for me, but he never did. My blood pressure stayed elevated, and I was bedridden. My childhood friend, family, co-workers, and some of the ladies from the church visited, but one evening my blood pressure was so high that I was not allowed to have any visitors.

CHAPTER 12

When I was still hospitalized during the last week of April, my mom began to get very concerned about my life. She met with the chief doctor and asked him why he did not take the baby by caesarean because I had been just lying there for too long. He informed her that the gynaecologist had advised that the baby was too small and she needed to give him at least two more weeks.

One week went by, and on April 29 when the nurse came to my bedside to do her checks, she told me to go catch a bath and then she would check my blood pressure again. When I came out of the shower, she came instantly and checked it, and then she checked the baby.

I saw her on the phone, and when the doctor arrived, I was told that they had to move me to the operating theatre to take the baby. I told my childhood friend to call my mom, and she came right away.

They prepped me for surgery and wheeled me away. Halfway to the theatre, I felt my whole body change, as if back to normalcy—as if I was no longer pregnant. I turned on my side and felt the baby flop to the side. I did it repeatedly, and then I began to cry. I knew the baby had died.

They took me back to the ward, and upon our arrival my mom asked why they had brought me back. I told her the baby was dead. It was so horrifying for me; here I am with a dead baby on the inside of me. I began wondering what was going to happen to me.

My mom told them to take the baby out of me before it killed me. They said they would put me on antibiotics but I would have to wait until it was time—it was ironic to me that it was the day before the baby was due, and that the baby would come out the day it was supposed to be born.

They sought ways of getting me to Nassau to have it removed but were told the same thing. So all I could do was lie there in the hospital bed until it was time. This was a sad time for me. I cried; after going through desertion and rejection, in the end the baby died. I questioned God and prayed to feel the baby kick again, but he never did. He just moved from side to side every time I did.

When the news spread around the island that Friday that my baby had died, a lot of people came to visit me especially those from the church. I remember a sister telling me that God had allowed this to happen to me for a reason and in the end I would see the reason why. I did not understand it, but it was a comfort at that moment because I was crying all the time.

I prayed to God to let this baby come out of me. Saturday went by, then when I woke that Sunday to take a shower, I noticed a discharge in my underwear and was told that the baby was ready to come out.

They instantly called my mom. She told an old nurse that she wanted her to be with me during the birth of this dead baby. I was heavily sedated for the birth. I was told that a lot of tears were shed for me that Sunday; I was also told that I spoke of my encounter with a person who had died, and therefore family and friends were worried that I was going to die.

That Sunday afternoon, May 1, 1988, I gave birth to a seven-pound, eight-ounce boy whom I named Denard Alonzo. About an hour after I gave birth, they brought him to my bedside for me to see. My mom had asked my dad to bury him early the next morning. I still can see his face with his pointed chin and a headful of coal black hair like my own and a mouth like his father's.

Since being hospitalized during my pregnancy, I never got a visit, a fruit, nor even a dollar from my baby's father. But that Sunday night, after all my family and friends left the hospital, he came walking into the maternity ward. I politely asked him what he wanted and said it was too late because the baby had died. He asked the nurse where he was, and she directed him. There he saw what would have been his son. After viewing the baby, he came to tell me he was leaving.

The next morning, the nurses on duty wrapped my son in a blanket. When my father came, he was placed in a box and taken away to be buried in the public cemetery. I remained hospitalized for three days afterward, with appointments to do follow-ups. Going home was the hardest thing. Leaving for home without my son, whom I came to love after carrying him for nine months, was very hard for me.

I instantly fell into a state of depression. I would sit for hours, holding his clothes, crying, and longing to have him in my arms. Early every morning I would find myself at the cemetery, crying at his grave, especially on Sundays. I never went unless I took flowers.

My condition worsened, and my mom told me to go away for the rest of my maternity leave. I went to the United States of America and the Bahamas for about two months.

I tried to take my mind off my problems, but I still cried when I think about my baby. He was the only thing I wanted.

CHAPTER 13

The time came for me to return home to my job. I went back to the Welfare Department and remained there for about two months. The position of secretary to the Chief Minister was vacant. My appointment to that position was a turning point in my life. While working in this position, the war started again at home. During that period, I made up my mind to fulfil my dream of living in Oklahoma and attending Oral Roberts University—and never come back home again.

Other persons had approached me to start a relationship, but after going through all the hurt and pain from my pregnancy and the rejection, I could never have done that. Deep inside I was still hoping for the return of my boyfriend. I had a terrible confrontation with him and his friend, and on January 1, 1989, on my way to the Old Year's Night service, I made up my mind that I would never look back that way again. I placed my life in God's hand to give me whomever He had for me.

I was reinstated into the church by writing a letter and apologizing for the sins I had committed. Back then, that's the way you were treated if you were to, as they termed it, "fall away." In a couple of months, I was given back my position as president in the Youth Department. I had lost the youth choir to another member of the church.

During the next few months, I began having dreams that I was walking in a garden, and while walking I met up with a young man who always took me by my hand. We never spoke to each other. We would just take a long walk, and then I would awake. I shared this recurring dream with a close friend of mine, and she told her mom about it. Her mom said that was the young man God had for me, and I was just to wait on the Lord.

About two months later, I was at work, and in walked this cool dark gentleman who was neatly dressed. I enquired as to who he was, and he introduced himself to me as my boss's cousin and said he had been hired as his driver.

Every day at work, my co-workers would tell me that this guy was going to be my boyfriend. I would argue with them, denying it all the time, but deep down inside I had the feeling that this was the guy I was seeing in my dream.

One day I was working late while a meeting was going on in the conference room. I had to attend to whatever files and refreshments might be needed in the meeting, and he and I were the only two left. We began to talk, and I found out more about who he was and where he was from.

From that evening on, over a month's time we talked and got to know each other. He invited me out on a date, then another, and from there we were in a relationship. I must admit it was a struggle for me, because I was not going to allow anyone to hurt me again.

We courted each other for over a year, and then he started telling me how he had come home to find a wife and that he wanted to marry me one day. Being on the rebound, I gave in to this sweet talk. As months went by I was again in active ministry, and found out I was pregnant.

I was so angry because I never wanted this to happen to me again. Because of the mistakes of my past, I felt horrible, and there I was slipping into depression. He was happy and excited when I told him I was pregnant, but I got angry because I was saying my life was ruined. After I told him all I had gone through, how could he have done this to me?

I did not speak to him for several days. and then one day he told me he was not going to leave me like my other boyfriend. He said he wanted to marry me, and he meant it.

When I went home that evening from work, my mom told me that he had come to her to say that he wanted to marry me. She said she agreed. He did not say anything to my father because he had never changed.

I went to my pastor and told him what was going on. I stepped down from my duties in the church, and we went into premarital counselling, which I found quite interesting. We began planning for the wedding from the day he told my mom. I must admit my mother was very supportive; she even accompanied me to Miami to shop for my special day.

My bridal party was planned, and everything was set. We were just waiting for the dresses to be made and the day to arrive. The time waiting for such an important day in a young girl's life usually would have been one of joy, but for me it was an eternal hell at home. My father said he was not going to walk me down the aisle. I felt so bad and cried. Then I was reminded that I had a brother whom I might like to do the honour for me. He consented and travelled home to be my father-giver.

I tried to endure all the physical and verbal challenges leading up to my wedding day, but it was hard. There I was, waiting to escape what I called torment for me.

CHAPTER 14

When May 26, 1990, came, it was a cool damp Saturday morning. At 7.30 a.m. the first bridesmaid began strutting up the church aisle. A hundred invited guests gazed upon each member of the wedding party as they took their place around the altar.

As I ascended from the car of a dear co-worker and friend of my husband, I felt like I was walking on air. My brother took me by the arm and on a journey I'd always remember. As I walked up the aisle, I could not believe I was the girl who had lived such a hard life and used to have such low self-esteem. As memories flooded my mind, I cried—not tears of sadness but of joy. My husband-to-be walked toward me and took me from my brother.

The ceremony was lovely, and my bridal party complemented me well, all decked in peach and beige, as I married someone whom I didn't love and who didn't love me. The church was lovely decorated, and we stood before our families who travelled from afar, friends and acquaintances, even the Governor, and pledged our love to each other.

Lots and lots of photos were taken, and then we were off to the reception, where the people who were special to us told us just how happy they were for us and wished us all the best. I will never forget the ambience of the place with the steeple cake and floral pieces.

That day we began our new lives together. I had made a vow to myself that I would make my home one of the happiest and make sure my child's life would not be like mine was.

We did not take a honeymoon then but went home for a time of relaxation until the other reception that was going to be held at my mom's residence was ready to begin. Despite the fact that this was our wedding day, the enemy was still working, determined that my life would be a living hell.

While my husband and I were sitting in the front room of the house we were living in, we saw a lady come into the yard, place a strange candle in the window, and run away. We went out and called after her, trying to find out where she got it or who gave it to her, but she was gone. We did not know what the candle in our window meant, but my new husband removed it and threw it away.

We left home later that evening to join our guests at the second reception at my mom's house. There was food, food, and more food, drinks, drinks, and more drinks. The cakes were laid on two large tables, and the many gifts we received were overwhelming. My cousins who came for the wedding made a listing of every gift, and the final count was one hundred and forty-seven.

The very next Sunday after our wedding, we invited our bridal party over for dinner as our way of saying thanks. Just after they had eaten, I began to get sick, with a pain in my stomach around my naval. My husband got worried and took me to the hospital. They called the doctor. I was treated and sent back home.

From that day, as my pregnancy progressed, I did not feel well at all. I was in and out of the hospital, with doctors saying that I was experiencing pre-labour pains.

CHAPTER 15

In August the pain had become so unbearable that I had to be rushed to the hospital from work. I stayed hospitalized for several days without getting any relief from the medication given to me, so we decided that I should seek medical attention abroad. The decision was to send me to Nassau.

The flight there was difficult. I had to travel through Miami, Florida, and didn't get into Nassau until about eleven that night. I was exhausted and feeling very sick.

I was to stay with my aunt, who is now deceased, while there in Nassau. The next day she took me to my doctor. I received a thorough exam, but because I was not having the pain at the time of my visit, it was difficult for my doctor to diagnose my problem. He told me to come to his office right away should the pain come back.

The following day I lay in bed all day, not feeling too well. My aunt gave me a delicious lunch of Kentucky Fried Chicken and fries. I enjoyed it very much, but right after eating it, I drifted off to sleep, only to awaken with the same sharp pain in my stomach around my navel. I took the same medication that the doctors in Grand Turk had given me, with the hope of getting relief but to no avail.

I told my aunt what was happening and that I needed to call my doctor's office to inform him of what was happening. It was almost closing time at his office, but he told me to come.

When I got there, he asked me to show him where I was experiencing the pain. I did, and he told me that I had an umbilical hernia and it was incarcerated. He turned to my aunt and said, "She needs surgery stat." He then phoned the emergency section of the hospital and instructed them that I was on my way and they must prep me for surgery right away to save my life and that of the baby.

I was nervous but relieved that I now knew what the problem was. Finally, I would get some relief.

We immediately left his office, and on his instructions my aunt took me straight to the hospital, before going to the house and getting my clothes. My aunt did as she was told, and when she went home she called my husband and my mother to let them know what was going on.

When my doctor arrived at the hospital, I was not ready for surgery, and he got irate with the nurses for not carrying out his instructions. But I was ready in less than an hour. He asked me if I had eaten that day, because you can't eat if you are going to have surgery. I told him what I had eaten, but he said he would have to monitor me closely because he could not take the risk of waiting for my body to digest and expel the food eaten. My doctor told the nurse to give me an enema to help, which she did.

As they were rolling me into the waiting area to go in the surgical theatre, my aunt arrived. I heard her talking to my doctor. He asked her why she brought so much baggage, and she told him it was my own and the baby's. "What baby?" he said to her. "That baby is going to stay right where it is until it's time to deliver."

"What?" she said.

"That's right!" he said.

I began to worry. After losing my first baby, I think it would have turned me crazy if I had lost this one. I began questioning myself about whether I should let them go on with the surgery. I had no choice, though, because of the pain. After that all I did was pray. I left it in God's hands because the doctor had said I could die.

That evening my faith got stronger than it's ever been. I trusted God to take care of me and the baby.

The next thing I remember after that is going in the surgical theatre and then out to the recovery room. When I opened my eyes, I vomited uncontrollably, but the doctors and nurses were standing by because they knew I had eaten before surgery and how dangerous it was. I was okay after that and was wheeled off to my bed.

My aunt was still there and stayed with me a while, then she left for home after I was settled and began to drift off to sleep.

The next morning my stomach pained me with a soreness that I'd never felt before. When my doctor came to my bedside, he told me that the surgery went well and that the hernia was huge. He explained to me that it was stopping the baby from being fed and it was also putting me in a dangerous position—I could have lost my life and that of the baby.

After being released from the hospital that Monday, I was instructed to attend clinic every day until the baby was due.

As my baby kicked and stretched in my stomach, especially at nights, all it did was hurt the cut I received from the surgery. I used to be so afraid that I would sit up in the bed with a pillow on my stomach, afraid that I would see little fingers poking out through the cut. The baby got so active after the surgery that my doctor said he too was beginning to fear that the baby would indeed push its fingers out.

The following day when I attended clinic, I heard my doctor make a noise when he examined my stomach. The baby had burst open two of the stitches! I was very scared. Until the incision healed, I would sit up and hold my stomach with the pillow continually.

Many nights I would put my little cassette player to my stomach for the baby to hear the music. I didn't know what effects it would have, but it was something I was inclined to do.

CHAPTER 16

It was the second week in October when I attended clinic. I was so frustrated and fatigued that I cried to my doctor to take the baby instead of letting it be born in its own time. He tried to comfort me, but it did me no good. He told me to wait another week, and if nothing happened he would make a decision. That week passed, and nothing did happen.

I went to clinic that next week and he told me I could write this date down in my diary: October 25. My baby would come into this world on that date. He said he would induce labour because of the medication and surgery which slowed down the baby.

I would ask him constantly whether I was having a boy or a girl, but he would always refuse to answer. It really didn't matter, though, because all I wanted was a healthy baby.

I phoned home to let my husband know, and he told my mom. It was decided that she would come to Nassau to be with me for the delivery because my husband was not able to come.

I anxiously waited for the twenty-fifth of October but was informed that my blood was very low. The last blood check that was done, it was a 5. My doctor said I was high risk, and I had to try to build up my blood with the help of iron tablets and other vitamins or I would be given a transfusion right before he induced labour. While I waited on the day to arrive, I ate blood-building foods, drank lots of V8 juice, Vita Malt, and a native tea called bras-lee-ta.

When the day came, I got up early and prepared myself. I had to be on the maternity ward at 10 a.m. for my blood check and the other formalities. I can praise the Lord that my blood was at 12 when they did the check.

As I was attending a private clinic, I had my own private nurses and private room. God had orchestrated everything for me; He gave me all professing Christians as my nurses, and this really made my journey so much easier. As I wept through the pain of childbirth, they held my hand and prayed and read the Word to me. If anyone had come on the ward that day, they never would have known I was experiencing childbirth pains. God helped me through it, though it was very painful.

The time came for me to deliver, and it was earlier than my doctor had anticipated. He had to be paged to the delivery room, where he came running in at full speed just as my baby was about to be born. He instructed me through the process. Knowing I was anaemic, he didn't want anything to go wrong that would cause me to begin bleeding. When a strong pain came, he told me to let this girl out. I did exactly that, and then I was presented with my beautiful baby girl, whom her dad and I named Tarina Bianca.

I distinctly remember the touch of her warm face against mine, and there and then we formed an even stronger bond than when she was in my womb. When I spoke to my husband over the phone right after that, he said to me, "Thank you for my daughter!" I could hear the joy in his voice. He was a proud father and still is to this day.

We left Nassau about two weeks later. I was anxious for her dad to see Tarina. When we reached Grand Turk, he was right there to meet us, and I presented him with his little queen. From the look on his face, one would have thought he was just presented with several million dollars. For me, it was so good to be back home after being away for three months.

CHAPTER 17

I am a firm believer that when a child is named, whatever characteristics that are attached to that name somehow attach to that person's personality. The name given to me by my parents derived from the Greek, *Barbara* meaning "stranger." I always felt and treated like a stranger among those who are supposed to be close to me.

As a married woman at the age of twenty-five, I might have thought everything would be okay, but as a result of how my life was during my formative years, challenges and ill treatment continued. Throughout the early years of marriage, I had a lot of illness that was neither medically explained nor treated. It was very frustrating for me to be sent abroad for treatment on numerous occasions, leaving my young child at home to be cared for by my family. It was not an easy period in my life.

I felt so tired from the constant pains in my chest, and not being able to breathe properly tormented me like a ghost living in a haunted house. I reached the point on two different occasions of just giving up during periods of illness, but it was not God's will. I remember distinctly one time when I had been sent to Princess Margret Hospital in Nassau. My body became numb, and I had movements only in my hands and face. I lay there and said to God, "Take me home! I am so tired!"

Then I heard a voice say to me, "Turn your head the other way!" I did, and there was my girl, Tarina, standing near the bed I was lying on as I awaited medical treatment for nine long hours. My girl was not there in person because she had been left at home; it was a sign for me not to give up, just for her.

After the doctors came over and examined me, they observed what was happening and I got medical care immediately. I was admitted for one week then released to go back home. As I came off the plane, my daughter, dressed in a red, yellow, and white dress, ran up to me with her arms outstretched, crying, "Oh my mommy, my mommy! Mommy, don't leave me no more!" That brought tears to my eyes, and I prayed and asked God to help me to live just for my daughter.

We found out later from a medical doctor that the sickness I was experiencing was not a normal one, and that he must seek help elsewhere. This was cause for concern to me. We knew exactly what he was telling us, and I was not willing to put my hands to evil. Whatever needed to be done God would have to do it. There are circumstances we are sometimes faced with in life that cause us to wonder how people can have such envy in their hearts toward you, to the extent that they will go the extra mile to try to destroy you.

I began to experience a funny sensation in my feet every time I would go into my yard to hang our clothes out to dry. It became so severe that one day my husband heard me screaming and came out to ask me what was wrong. I told him. He grew concerned and said he was going to do what the doctor told him.

I don't know what he did, but earlier on that day, I'd been telling a co-worker of mine about my experiences and what this doctor told us we needed to do. A man of God was visiting a church, and I'd decided to go there one night. As the prophet was praying for people, he told me to come; he wanted to pray with me. When I got there, this gentleman told me my entire life story and what I was experiencing, then whispered in my ear who was doing these things to me.

My co-worker who was at the service didn't see me in front of the prophet because a lot of other people were there. But she told me the next day that as he was speaking, she said to her sister, "Barbie was telling how those same things happened to her today!"

Then her sister said to her, "Barbie is who he's talking to!" She said how that made her shiver.

When I returned home and told my husband what had happened, he told me he knew but didn't want to tell me who it was. I asked him what he did, and he said "Nothing! But no one can harm you!"

As years went by, I came to find out the entire story and how it stemmed from the candle placed in our window on our wedding day. That failed, but then a bottle was planted under my clothesline; a pair of pants was given to me, which I burned up; and finally a bar of soap was given to me, which I placed in the garbage.

My final bout of that type of illness placed me in an Aztec, a two-seater plane that flew me to Jamaica. That was scary, as we flew near Haiti. I became extremely ill but made it safely and was admitted to the University Hospital of the West Indies, where I got good health care. I was treated and returned home. I am now free of that, and I give God all the glory for taking good care of me. We were told later on that the witchcraft originated out of Haiti, and that was why I got so ill.

CHAPTER 18

As a young lady growing up, I had such a rough life. Running away to school and then getting married was my way of escaping all the abuse and hurt I suffered. Looking back, I came to realize that life is a journey. While on this journey, we as human beings sometimes think that what we choose is what has been ordained or predestined for our lives. I am convinced also that sometimes we are so anxious to escape what is happening to us that we follow our own minds instead of waiting on God no matter how many years it may take, and consequently we ourselves may cause more havoc in our lives.

As I look back, I got married at such a young age because of my stand as a Christian and what others might say, marrying someone I hardly knew and didn't love, but because of the pregnancy, I hastily got married before getting to know the individual a little more. My advice to both young adults and older persons is to be certain that you are truly in love with the person you intend to marry, because later on the lack of love can have adverse effects on your emotional, spiritual, and physical lives.

For many years of my life during that period, I met with a lot of hardships that I will not detail. It became so bad that I began falling back into not loving myself. The low self-esteem began to resurface. I didn't care anymore about myself, my appearance, or my life. This was not the dream I had for my life. Entering into a marriage not loving with the hope of getting to love is a big gamble. There was no way I could have loved because of the circumstances of the emotional and verbal abuse I suffered for years.

I began to think that this was my fate in life. I asked God one day, "Am I going to die in this state of living and not yet having lived?" Life brought me to the brink of not wanting to live once again.

I found myself always wanting to make things right in my relationships in all aspects. I sought counsel from a pastor on another island, too ashamed to let anyone close to me know what I was going through for so many years.

After seeking the necessary help, I was asked for a divorce. I was told that I wasn't wanted anymore. Being a faithful and dutiful person, I felt rejected and had to find a way out, which I did after years of no affection whatsoever but remaining faithful. The situation got so bad that I was disappointed when I was still going to face another day of life. I think this brought me to reality.

After seeking advice, I took the next step with much difficulty and hardship. At that point in my life, I hit rock-bottom and felt like there was no end in sight.

During my years of difficulties, I never told anyone what I was going through. I suffered for years in silence. Here I am, pastoring a church, serving God during my years of suffering—how would it sound when people hear of me getting divorced? What will people say? This is something I had to face and didn't know what it would be like. It was going to either make or break me.

The first request to read and sign came with another series of hardships for me. Each time, I was left feeling as if I was beaten physically. I reached the point where I would have preferred being beaten because of the effect it was having on me mentally and emotionally.

One morning it was all signed and sealed, and I was on the road for an even rougher ride. The year 2014 was one of the saddest and most difficult years of my life—going through a divorce as a pastor, people surprised at the news because from the outside it looked like I had a happy life.

During that time, I fell into a state of depression. Unable to sleep or eat, I survived by drinking smoothies and water each day. I didn't sleep for nights on end as I lay there soaking my pillow with tears. Inside, I felt like I was literally dying. The talk around the island—among persons who had absolutely no idea of what I endured—blamed me and insinuated that I was the one at fault, that I was the one who asked for the divorce. I walked alone for two long years.

I revealed to a few what I went through for years, and they were surprised and asked why I never said anything. I never would have said anything about what I was going through because there was no one there for me, no one I could really trust who would have listened to me without judging me. Years of being made to feel like a nobody drove me into an even greater shell. I felt like no one loved nor cared for me.

Sometimes I can't help thinking about all the hurt, pain, and disappointments I have had to endure in my life and the fact that I was living a lie. Living a life of constant torment and loneliness, I can only say, "If it had not been for the Lord on my side, not only would I have already lost my mind, but I probably would have been sleeping in my cold, lifeless grave. But God!"

In recent years, just as I have done in prior years, I tried to find other ways and means of escaping what I was going through. However, I believe that everything happens for a reason, and at the end of the day, all things work together for the good of those who love the Lord and are called according to His purpose. There are times when we see each other from day to day and it seems that everything is fine and dandy in others' lives, but I have come to a place where I truly believe "never judge the book by the cover."

There are times when I feel myself getting in a slump and going into a dark pit. So as a means of escape, I preoccupy myself with my passion, youth work. I count it a blessing to have been afforded the opportunity on numerous occasions to engage in the work of the Government's Ministry of Youth, travelling within the Turks and Caicos Islands to meet with international organizations such as UNICEF and the Commonwealth Youth Program, and to help formulate policies and programs for the youth of these Islands. My years of experience in this field has provided opportunities which have not only helped the youth but been therapeutic to me in the process.

I have not allowed the negative and depressing aspects of my life to overshadow me and impede my progress in life. Instead I created other escape routes. In so doing, I have taken every opportunity to further my education by acquiring both certifications in human resource management and finance from Florida Atlantic University in the United States, and a certification in management by the UK's National School of Government.

In addition to preoccupying myself with youth work and academic studies in an effort to bury that dreadful season of my life and perhaps solve my problems, I engaged in reading articles on marriage, such as "The Magic of Intimacy." The promise of marriage lies in its ability to mend our wounds. Our most intimate relationships are often therapeutic; they're able to rehabilitate us psychologically and emotionally. Marriage encourages us to expose ourselves to our partners and lay bare our weaknesses, and in so doing our lovers become agents of healing.

Despite the fact that I was on the rebound when I met my husband and needed a way to escape what I was experiencing at that time, I never loved him. I told myself that with time I would grow to love him. A dear friend of mine shared the same opinion and encouraged me to proceed with the wedding. I believe that there are couples who may have made the same mistake I did years ago, but their personalities and the way their partners treated them may have led them to love. Unfortunately, that was not the case for me.

After suffering so much psychological and emotional trauma over the years, I found myself going through the same struggle over and over again and pretending that I was happy and everything was great. Besides not loving him, I was living such a lonely life physically that I yearned to be loved and touched in a loving, caring, and passionate way.

When people try to endure an unhappy marriage, most of the time it's for the sake of commitment and to honour marriage vows they made; and then there are those who will fight for the relationship because they believe in it—they see a future and aren't ready to give up on the history they've created together.

So I ask this question: when you've tried for so many years to build a happy and healthy marriage and nothing happens, should you jump and abandon it, continue to fight for it even though you know you are fighting a losing battle, or hold onto the understanding that marriages are imperfect and go through rough patches but might settle down and improve? And how do you factor your children into the equation?

There is no single clear-cut path to follow that is guaranteed to lead to the right outcome. How I resolve this dilemma will psychologically depend on my personal circumstances and the conclusions I reach through a lot of thought. Do I continue to suffer sexually and emotionally? What I am to do? My mind goes to the book of Corinthians where the Apostle Paul admonishes the church at Corinth that it is better to marry then to burn. If I was given the chance to speak with Paul now, my question to him would be, "What if you're married yet you're still burning?" I wonder what his godly answer would be.

Time ticks on, and there's no universal law telling me what to do; it's truly my choice. Time ticks on, and our child values the fact that her parents are together despite her mother's pain. Time ticks on, and I am stuck in an arid relationship while stewing in regret. Time ticks on as every day I try to make the decision to stay or leave. Time ticks on, and no one can predict the future.

I've come to realize that in times of emotional crisis, there is an opportunity to grow and learn. Feeling emptiness in my life doesn't mean that nothing is happening or that things will never change. In the end, based on whatever the decision will be, I want to emerge from this experience knowing myself better and feeling even stronger.

In May of that year, I was asked for the divorce. It was filed in June and granted the first week in September.

Life ahead for me was scary. I didn't know what my life was going to be like as a single woman. I was told that no one would love me and that I was a nobody. I cried out to God every night. I ended up right back in that place I was in in my younger years.

I just couldn't do it anymore. I couldn't face what I was facing anymore. As a result, after dropping my daughter at work one morning I decided to drive to the beach and end it all. I was going into the sea and putting my head under and killing myself.

Whilst sitting in my Jeep, I heard the voice of God speaking to me, asking me what my daughter would say and how she would feel when I did not pick her up, and when I could not be found or my body was found floating dead. I broke down in tears, started up my Jeep, and went back home.

I spoke with a friend who told me to listen to the Word at night and to mediate, which I started doing. I wrote many articles at night, which I called "Midnight Meditations." I began to mend day by day. Then I went to a women's empowerment conference where I got my breakthrough and new lease on life.

Whilst going through a divorce can be a difficult and painful experience, moving on from it felt like an impossible task. However, with time, patience, and the right mind-set, it is possible to heal and start anew once you've made up your mind to move on after a painful divorce.

I had to allow myself to grieve. Divorce is a significant loss, a loss of so many wasted years of your life—for me, more than twenty years. It felt normal to feel sad, angry, and disappointed. I never once didn't allow myself to feel those emotions and didn't try to suppress them. I cried, and I had a friend I spoke to. At first, I felt in my spirit that she didn't understand or didn't think I was being honest about some of the things I told her I went through because I had never told anyone. It was so important to acknowledge my feelings so that I could process them and move forward.

My divorce was emotionally and physically draining, so it was essential to take care of myself, even though I lost a lot of weight. Sleep was far from me, but I made sure to exercise regularly, eat healthy food such as smoothies, and try to reduce the stress. Some days I felt very weak, but the more I took care of myself, the better I felt and the more strength I regained.

One thing I had to learn was to let go of the past. It's easy to get stuck in the past and obsess over what could have been, but dwelling on the past was only going to prevent me from moving forward. Instead, I focused on the present and the future. I accepted the fact that I wasn't loved and that the relationship was over. I forgave myself for staying all those years, and I forgave him; I let go of all the resentment and bitterness.

I felt lost and unsure of who I was at first, but as time went by, I started to rediscover my identity. I took that opportunity to rediscover myself. I pursued hobbies and interests I've always wanted to try. Rediscovering my identity helped me feel more confident and fulfilled.

CHAPTER 19

Church and ministry life for me started when I was nine years old and first accepted Jesus as my personal Lord and Saviour. I knew I was called by God from my young years. I used to have dreams of myself preaching in front of large crowds. I saw myself active in ministry before it began.

Throughout my life in ministry, I have served as praise and worship leader, youth leader, choir director, and director of the fine arts ministry. I was first ordained as youth pastor, after which I became district youth pastor, associate pastor, and assistant pastor.

Life for me in the church was a struggle. I was met with great opposition and backlash. At every church I served in, there were times when I allowed the Lord to use me but the spirit of jealousy presented itself. Once when I was ministering to a young lady at the altar, a leader took the microphone from me because she felt like I was outdoing the pastor, who was not present. I've had microphones lowered and cut off whilst ministering. I've been overlooked to lead, rejected, and used just to make ministries look good.

I never allow any of this ungodly treatment I receive from "church" folks to deter me from serving God. I know He gifted me with gifts to be used in His kingdom. But it's amazing to know that even in the place where you should feel wanted and appreciated, you feel like dirt. Can you imagine? People will sit in the pulpit with you and, if you are called on to pray, won't even say amen when you're done, let alone say it whilst you're preaching God's word.

Many times I wondered, "Lord, when will this end for me? When will I be used in Your church freely without this type of ungodly behaviour from Christians?"

A holding pattern is not a place I like to be in, but it seems as if God is preparing me for something greater. I thank God for the years I served in the youth ministry. His Word says, "Bring forth fruit and let it remain." I can say that by allowing God to use me, there was fruit in the form of pastors, youth pastors, youth ministers, youth preachers, singers, musicians, praise dancers, and youth leaders, all for the glory and honour of God. Another area in ministry that's very effective is speaking into the lives of women at women's gatherings and conferences. I am a servant of God to work in His kingdom for His glory, bringing men, women, boys, and girls to Him. It's all about Him, not me.

In Christian circles, being a divorcee made me feel inferior. The people around me made me feel like a failure, as if I should have stayed in the abuse of many years. I'd hear statements like, "I went through so much with my husband, and … ." Having been around these people before my divorce, I had not heard these types of conversations until then. They really made me feel like a castaway. I asked myself, "Who are they to judge me? Do they know what I endured?" I endured stuff that I will not share with anyone, but God knows what I went through, and it is He I have to give an account to.

The ridicule became unbearable. Having to face a lot of ridicule was a very devastating experience for me that had me feeling humiliated, rejected, and isolated. It was especially difficult to cope with when it came from people who I cared about or respected. As time went on, however, I've learnt strategies that can help overcome the negative effects of ridicule and move forward with confidence and resilience.

I now understand that ridicule is a form of social rejection that involves mocking or belittling someone in a way that causes them to feel humiliated or embarrassed. It can be verbal or nonverbal, and can take many different forms, including teasing, sarcasm, and mockery. Ridicule can be intentional or unintentional, and can be perpetrated by individuals or groups, some of whom might surprise you. Ridicule had a profound impact on my self-esteem and sense of identity. It caused me feelings of shame, anxiety, and depression, and led me to withdraw from social interaction. It also led me to suicidal ideation.

There are several strategies that individuals can use to cope with ridicule and move forward with resilience. Today I would advise anyone who faces ridicule to reframe the situation rather than internalizing the ridicule. Don't assume it reflects something negative about yourself. It can be helpful to reframe the situation in a more positive light. This might involve considering the motivations of the individual or group perpetrating the ridicule, or recognizing that the ridicule says more about the person doing the ridiculing than the person being ridiculed. This is something I had to learn.

If you can, seek some support. I am happy that God placed a few persons in my circle to support me. I find that talking about the experience with someone who is understanding and supportive can help you process your feelings and develop a plan for moving forward.

I remember being very hard on myself. I was almost at the point of feeling like I deserved it and I was to blame, when of course I was not. I had to reach a point where I could practice self-compassion rather than being harsh and critical with myself. Practicing self-compassion involves treating yourself with kindness and understanding, and recognizing that everyone makes mistakes and experiences setbacks. Bad things do happen to good people.

I reached a point of taking action by speaking up and representing myself. Take action to address a situation might involve confronting the individual or group perpetrating the ridicule, which I did, addressing it in a way that helped me take steps to improve my self-esteem and resilience.

My season of ridicule was a challenging experience, but there were strategies I used to overcome its negative effects. I recognized the source of the ridicule; I reframed the situation; I confided in my small circle and stopped being hard on myself. In so doing, I was able to move forward with confidence and resilience.

CHAPTER 20

Almost three years later after the separation, life for me changed for the better. One Sunday morning in church as we were greeting each other, I greeted a man with whom I felt a connection. It was weird. In church? Yes! He and I became acquaintances for a while. Our conversations progressed to long hours on the phone, talking about life and our various struggles, which were similar.

Love, which was far from my mind and life, came alive. But I became afraid of another relationship. I questioned God. Would I be sinning? Would I be punished? What will God see this as?

Throughout my enduring the bad experience, I had asked God if I was going to die without having the heaven on earth of being happy and having a husband who loved me and whom I loved. I now asked God to prove to me that this was what He wanted for my life by giving me the opportunity to travel to another island for an individual's birthday. I was surprised when the opportunity presented itself that very same day for me to travel to that island overnight. This was something that I didn't take lightly.

We spent the evening in a quiet restaurant, eating a meal together to celebrate his birthday. After the meal I presented him with a gift. I was not at the place yet where a relationship had to be formed. I knew how hard life was for him, and therefore I made it my choice to make him feel special.

After we left for our respective homes, I had a lot of thoughts going through my mind. On the flight back home the next morning, I talked to God again about it and wanted Him to decide for me.

After talking and fellowshipping for about three months, we decided to give it a try. My mind was filled with questions. Will I be treated the way I was treated? How will this work out? Marriage was nowhere on our minds. Just companionship. Someone to talk to.

A year later, my job transferred me to the island where he lives. I didn't mind because I needed to start over and to get away from the island talk. Making that move meant giving up the leadership of the church, which wasn't hard at all because I didn't feel wanted nor appreciated there.

Leaving my daughter and my home was a tough thing to do, but I knew I had to. Even though she and I were just twenty minutes apart, I cried many days from missing her badly. I felt like I abandoned her. I felt guilty leaving her alone—even though she was almost thirty years old, she was still my baby, my only child.

After almost four years of being divorced, here I was again. We decided to get married and build a life together. Telling my daughter was my biggest fear. I wondered what her response would be. When I broke the news to her, she was excited. She said she was happy for me and wanted me to be happy. That was all I needed.

Being married again has fulfilled my dream of the type of life I wanted for myself. A life of togetherness, love, and friendship. What we've built together in almost seven years I wasn't able to do in the more than twenty years I consider in some sense wasted and yet a path I trod to get me to where I am today.

CHAPTER 21

Many of us speak of "what we are going through," but the good news is that going *through* it means we are not stuck in our troubles with no way out. I am now a firm believer that God never promises us trouble-free lives but does promise to be with us and never to leave or forsake us. When God takes us through something, it is not for us all the time. What we go through is His road map to get us to where He wants us to be. God will always teach us valuable lessons that we can use in the future.

I've had hardships throughout most of my life, but there were a few years that were most challenging. The challenges I have overcome have taught me how to look at obstacles in a different way. Instead of saying "Why me?" I now say, "Why not me?"

Throughout most of my life, I walked down a very lonely and dark path, and the only person I can give praise to for bringing me through is God. I am still met with circumstances that could cause me to want to give up and digress, but I know better now; it's just a pathway to greatness. One of the most important times to hear from God is when we need direction as we go through difficulties. Trusting God to help us will keep us from giving up in the midst of our difficulties.

The first year after moving, I decided to fulfil one of my dreams: graduating with a bachelor's degree in human resource management, which I acquired with a 4.0 grade point average. After obtaining my bachelor's, I went on to pursue my master's. With the support and encouragement of my husband, I was able to complete it, even though I wanted to give up many times.

In my life and ministry, the love of preaching the word of God is most important in my life. I've served many years in churches and have been met with much disappointment and hardship, but I made a promise that after I completed my master's, the only other studying I would do is theology, which I did, embracing the opportunity. I can now say that I've obtained my doctorate in theology.

After all these years of trauma and abuse, I can truly say that I am a stronger person than I was back then. I've come to realize that each day given to us is meant to live happily, despite what we as individuals may be faced with. I am coming to realize also that in the end my standing with Christ and my happiness should be of the utmost importance. Whenever I encounter people or situations that will take my peace, I disassociate myself.

In reality, all those years when I stayed, afraid of really living, I allowed my heart to be vandalized. In this life, many women and men live from day to day, allowing their hearts to be trampled on.

Many of us were dropped at some point in our lives—be it by a spouse, parent, sibling, fellow Christian or pastor, organization or community—and we all have the choice to either get up or stay down. Now and then we have to take an inventory of ourselves. We should not live each day without enjoying the life that God has destined for us. Many are afraid of ridicule and what people might say, as I was back then and even today; but a time in your life must come when you separate yourself from people or things that are not adding happiness to your life. God wants us to live abundant lives. It is not His desire for us to live in turmoil.

As individuals going through the storms of life, we ought to use those seasons as a pathway to the purpose which God has destined for our lives.

CHAPTER 22

We all must realize that we each have a unique journey we are on, and sometimes we may find ourselves feeling lost or unsure of where we are headed. But I want to encourage you today that God is always with us, leading us on the path that He has prepared for us, not what we want for ourselves.

Proverbs 3:5–6 says, "Trust in the Lord with all your heart and lean not on your own understanding; in all your ways submit to him, and he will make your paths straight." This means that we must trust in God's plan for our lives, even when we don't fully understand it. We must submit to His will and follow His lead, knowing that He will guide us to where we need to be.

The pathway that God has for us may not be easy. It may be filled with challenges and obstacles that we must overcome. But we must remember that God uses these difficulties to shape us and prepare us for His purpose. Romans 8:28 says, "And we know that in all things God works for the good of those who love him, who have been called according to his purpose."

Today when I face hardships, I can trust that God is working everything together for my good. We all must have faith that God's ways are higher than our ways and that He has a plan for our lives that is greater than we could ever imagine. I am a living testimony of that.

In Jeremiah 29:11, " 'For I know the plans I have for you,' declares the Lord, 'plans to prosper you and not to harm you, plans to give you hope and a future.' " This means that God has a specific purpose for each of our lives, and He wants us to succeed and thrive. We must trust that He will guide us on the path that will lead us to this purpose.

My pathway was filled with physical, sexual, emotional, and verbal abuse. I've had hardships of lack and loneliness. Today I look at trials as steps to the something greater which God has destined for my life. We must trust in God's plan for our lives, even when it may not make sense to us. I've learned to submit to His will and follow His lead, knowing that He is always with me, guiding me on the path that He has prepared for me.

Finding your purpose while on a pathway of pain and abuse can be a challenging and difficult journey, but it is possible. Despite the difficulties, it is important to remember that you are not defined by your past experiences, and that your current circumstances do not have to dictate your future.

I realize now that the first step towards finding your purpose is to seek help and support for the pain and abuse that you are experiencing. This may involve reaching out to a therapist, which I did later on. I regret not confiding in a trusted friend or family member. I've learned that it is important to prioritize your mental and emotional well-being, as healing from past traumas is an essential part of moving forward.

Today, I tell everyone who may have gone through some of what I went through that once you have taken steps to address your pain and abuse, you can begin to explore your passions and interests. Take some time to reflect on what brings you joy and fulfilment, and consider how you can incorporate these things into your daily life. This may involve exploring new hobbies, doing something that you are passionate about, or pursuing a career that aligns with your values and interests.

Be patient and compassionate with yourself throughout this process. Remember that finding your purpose is a journey, and it may take time to discover what truly resonates with you. Celebrate your small successes and accomplishments along the way, as they can serve as motivators to continue moving forward.

On your pathway surround yourself with positivity and encouragement. Seek out people who support and uplift you, and distance yourself from those who bring negativity or toxicity into your life. Remember that you deserve to live a life filled with purpose, happiness, and fulfilment, and that you have the power to create that reality for yourself.

If you're facing a rough time in your life, I want you to remember that this too shall pass. Remember that difficult times are temporary and will eventually come to an end. You will get through this even though you may feel at times like it is never going to be over.

Tell yourself that you are strong. You have the strength within you to overcome any obstacle or challenge that comes your way. Believe in yourself and your ability to persevere.

One thing I can tell you is that you are not alone. If no one is with you, God is. Even when it seems like He is not, hope in God. Trust Him when you cannot trace Him. Reach out to your loved ones and or a close friend who will be your support system, people who care about you and want to help you through this tough time.

I found that I had to take care of myself. Self-care is important, especially during difficult times. Take time to do things that make you feel good and bring you peace, whether it's exercising, meditating, reading, or spending time with loved ones.

I've learned from this experience, and you can also. Sometimes difficult times can teach us important lessons about ourselves and our lives. Look for the silver lining and try to learn from this experience so that you can grow and become stronger. Remember, you are not defined by your struggles. You are a strong, resilient, and capable individual who will overcome this rough patch. Keep pushing forward and don't give up hope.

Finding your purpose in life can be a challenging and sometimes frustrating journey, but remember that it is possible and completely within your reach. In order to stay on the path, you have to keep on exploring. Finding your purpose is a process that takes time and exploration. You can't be afraid to try new things and to step outside your comfort zone. Keep exploring different interests, passions, and hobbies until you find what truly speaks to your soul; most important, seek God's guidance.

Trust God and listen to that inner voice that knows what you want and what you are meant to do. Trust and follow your intuition as you explore different paths and opportunities.

Whilst on your pathway you have to embrace failure. It's okay to stumble and fall along the way. Failure is a natural part of the process and can teach you important lessons that will help you in the long run. Don't let setbacks discourage you from pursuing your purpose. I had many, but I did not let myself stop.

One of the main things I had to do was maintain a positive mindset, which I found was crucial when searching and seeking God for my purpose in life. I tried to only focus on my strengths. Every now and then I celebrated my accomplishments, and now I always surrounds myself with positivity.

CHAPTER 23

After years of twists, turns, ups, downs, pain, and suffering, I've finally begun to walk in the purpose that God has for my life.

Finding one's purpose is a lifelong quest that shapes our existence, gives meaning to our actions, and fuels our passion for life. Knowing your purpose is just as important as walking in the pathway that God has for you. For me, it is a journey of self-discovery that empowers me to live more intentionally, find fulfilment, and contribute positively to those around me and the world.

Over the years I've realized that understanding your purpose is not a one-size-fits-all endeavour; it is deeply personal and unique to each individual. It often involves introspection, self-reflection, and a commitment to living authentically.

Knowing your purpose provides a compass for life. It offers a clear direction, guiding you through the ups and downs, and helping you make decisions that align with your core values and passions. Once I became in tune with my purpose, I'm experiencing a sense of inner peace and contentment.

Having a sense of purpose also fuels my motivation to work out my purpose. I realize that when you wake up with a clear understanding of why you do what you do, you find the determination to overcome obstacles and stay committed to your goals. It's a source of resilience in the face of any adversity you may face.

Now that I know and began to walk in my purpose, I now foster a profound sense of fulfilment. It allows me to engage in activities and pursuits that resonate with my soul. This, in turn, enhances my overall well-being, contributing to my physical, mental, and emotional health.

The benefits of knowing my purpose extends beyond my personal growth. It empowers me to make a positive impact on those around me and the world. As I align my actions with my purpose, I'm becoming a force for good, inspiring and uplifting those around me every day.

Over the years, even in the midst of my suffering I preached many sermons, spoke at various women's conferences and retreats which impacted the lives of many. Setting the bar for others by walking away from emotional and verbal abuse caused me to be able to counsel many. You have to learn to love yourself, you have to at one point in your life to "do you" whilst being whom God has called you to be.

Women's empowerment was birth through all that I went through. As I embark on this ministry it is aimed at propelling others to walk in their purpose.

Beauty for Ashes Women, which is a ministry that God has inspired me to establish, is an arm of Charisma Evangelistic Ministry formed by me over twenty years ago. As I feed children and assist those that are in need, counselling hurting women, preaching the word of God, is only a fraction of fulfilling my purpose.

My prayer to God each day is, "In my life Lord, be glorified!" This is my purpose, to bring glory to God and not myself.

As you're on your pathway, you must keep moving forward, because finding your purpose is a journey, not a destination. I had to keep moving forward, one step at a time, and never gave up on myself.

I now have faith that no matter what I am faced with, God's purpose for my life is greater than I can ever imagine!

Finding your purpose is a rewarding and fulfilling experience. I always told myself, "stay focused, stay true to yourself, and keep pushing forward. You've got this!"

As my pathway to my purpose continues, I am now living, loving, and laughing!

To God be all the glory!

Printed in the United States
by Baker & Taylor Publisher Services